PRAYERS
■ OF THOSE ■
WHO MAKE MUSIC

LITURGY
TRAINING
PUBLICATIONS

Acknowledgments

The translation of the psalms copyright © 1994; excerpt from the Exultet, copyright © 1973; excerpts from the *Book of Blessings,* copyright © 1987; by the International Committee on English in the Liturgy, Inc.

Scripture passages are taken from the New Revised Standard Version, copyright © 1989, Division of Christian Education, National Council of the Churches of Christ in the United States of America.

"A Prayer for Musicians," and "A Prayer for Singers," from *The Book of Occasional Services,* copyright © 1979 by Church Pension Fund. Used by permission.

All quotes of Alice Parker from *Melodious Accord: Good Singing in Church,* copyright © 1991 by Liturgy Training Publications.

Excerpts from *The Reed of God* and *The Flowering Tree* by Caryll Houselander, copyright © 1947, 1954 by Sheed and Ward.

Excerpt from "Music in the Black Spiritual Tradition," by G. W. Brown in *This Far by Faith,* copyright © 1977 by The Liturgical Conference.

Excerpt from "Music, The Way of Return," by Herbert Whone, from *Parabola,* (vol. 5, no. 2), copyright © 1980, The Society for the Study of Myth and Tradition.

Excerpts from *The Insecurity of Freedom,* by Abraham Heschel, copyright © 1966 by Farrar, Straus and Giroux.

Excerpt from *The Oath,* by Elie Wiesel, copyright © 1973 by Random House.

Excerpt from *Prayers, Poems and Songs,* by Huub Oosterhuis, copyright © 1970 by Herder and Herder.

Excerpt from *Life Together,* by Dietrich Bonhoeffer, copyright © 1954 by Harper and Row.

"Prayer of the Saints Who Make Music," written and copyrighted by David Philippart. All rights reserved. Used with permission.

Excerpt from "The Gift of African American Sacred Song," by Thea Bowman, in *Lead Me, Guide Me,* copyright © 1987 by GIA Publications.

Excerpt from "Lift Every Voice and Sing," by James W. Johnson, copyright © 1921 by Edward B. Marks Music Company.

"Earth and all stars," by Herbert Brokering, copyright © 1968 by Augsburger Publishing House.

Excerpt from "When Love is Found," by Brian Wren, copyright © 1983, Hope Publishing Company.

Excerpt from "To the Composer," copyright © 1977 by John Combs.

Excerpt from *Music in Catholic Worship,* by the Bishops' Committee on the Liturgy, copyright © 1972 by the United States Catholic Conference.

Excerpt from *How Can I Keep From Singing,* by Gabe Huck, copyright © 1989, Liturgy Training Publications.

"When in our music God is glorified," by F. P. Green, copyright © 1972, Hope Publishing Company.

This book was compiled by David Philippart, with assistance from Alan Lukas and Pedro A. Vélez. It was designed by Anna Manhart and typeset in Galliard by Karen Mitchell. Andrew Manhart did the artwork. *Prayers of Those Who Make Music* was printed in the United States of America.

Copyright © 2004, 1999, 1995, Archdiocese of Chicago: Liturgy Training Publications, 1800 North Hermitage Avenue, Chicago IL 60622-1101; 1-800-933-1800; FAX 1-800-933-7094; E-MAIL orders@ltp.org. All rights reserved.

Visit our website at www.ltp.org.

04 03 02 01 00   7 6 5 4 3

Library of Congress Catalog Card Number 95-81726
ISBN 1-56854-131-7
MUSICR

Sing a new song, you faithful,
praise God in the assembly.
Israel, rejoice in your maker,
Zion, in your king.
Dance in the Lord's name,
sounding harp and tambourine.

   —Psalm 149:1–3

Shout joy to the Lord, all earth,
serve the Lord with gladness,
enter God's presence with joy!

Know that the Lord is God,
our maker to whom we belong,
our shepherd, and we the flock.

Enter the temple gates,
the courtyard with thanks and praise;
give thanks and bless God's name.

Indeed the Lord is good!
God's love is for ever,
faithful from age to age.

—*Psalm 100*

The priests came out of the holy place (for all the priests who were present had sanctified themselves, without regard to their divisions, and all the levitical singers, Asaph, Heman, and Jeduthun, their sons and kindred, arrayed in fine linen, with cymbals, harps and lyres, stood east of the altar with 120 priests who were trumpeters). It was the duty of the trumpeters and singers to make themselves heard in unison in praise and thanksgiving to the LORD, and when the song was raised, with trumpets and cymbals and other musical instruments, in praise to the LORD,

> "For he is good,
> for his steadfast love endures forever,"

the house, the house of the LORD, was filled with a cloud, so that the priests could not stand to minister because of the cloud; for the glory of the LORD filled the house of God.

—*2 Chronicles 5:11–14*

A Prayer for Musicians

When the song was raised in the praise of the
    Lord:
The glory of the Lord filled the house of God.

O God, whom saints and angels delight to worship in heaven, be ever present with your servants who seek through music to perfect the praises offered by your people on earth and grant them even now glimpses of your beauty, and make them worthy at length to behold it unveiled for evermore: through Jesus Christ our Lord. Amen.

— *The Book of Occasional Services*

A Prayer for Singers

O God, who inspired David the king both to write songs and to appoint singers for your worship: Give grace to the singers in your church, that with psalms, and hymns, and spiritual songs, they may sing and make music to the glory of your name, through Jesus Christ our Lord. Amen.

— *The Book of Occasional Services*

When the horses of pharaoh with his chariots and his chariot drivers went into the sea, the LORD brought back the waters of the sea upon them, but the Israelites walked through the sea on dry ground.

Then the prophet Miriam, Aaron's sister, took a tambourine in her hand, and all the women went out after her with tambourines and with dancing. And Miriam sang to them:

> "Sing to the LORD, for he has triumphed gloriously;
> horse and rider he has thrown into the sea."

—*Exodus 15:19–21*

With joy I heard them say,
"Let us go to the Lord's house!"
And now, Jerusalem,
we stand inside your gates.

Jerusalem, the city so built
that city and temple are one.

To you the tribes go up,
every tribe of the Lord.

It is the law of Israel
to honor God's name.
The seats of law are here,
the thrones of David's line.

Pray peace for Jerusalem:
happiness for your homes,
safety inside your walls,
peace in your great houses.

For love of family and friends
I say, "Peace be with you!"
For love of God's own house
I pray for your good.

—*Psalm 122*

A Song Does Not Exist

A song does not exist until it is sung, or re-created, by a human voice. Every incarnation is different, and no one sound is the only right one. This is a paradox. A page of music seems to present a finished product, yet it contains no sound. (Hold it up to your ear: Can you hear it?) The song doesn't live until it comes off of the page and resumes its natural state as sound. The page can no more substitute for living sound than a recipe can for edible food.

—*Alice Parker*

The Love Song of God

In the beginning the love song of God
    is a folk song.
Folk song is the telling of the whole world's story
    through the singing of one's heart.
The word of God uttered in Christ's human life
    is a folk song.

In it is all the primal love and joy
    and sorrow of all the world.
We hear it as children playing by the seashore hear
    the music of the ocean in a little shell.
We hear it in the voices we know best: our own
    children's voices, the voices of our parents,
    wives, husbands and friends.
We hear it in laughter and tears, tuned to the
    fullness of our hearing, tuned
    to the beating of our hearts.
We hear it as sweet and clear
    as a bird's song in Nazareth.
The song of the Incarnation is a folk song.
It is the song of the mother rocking the cradle.
It is the song of the children singing
    their nursery rhymes.
It is the song of the shepherd calling his sheep.
It is the song of the lover standing at the door.
It is the song of the bridegroom
    singing to the bride.

—*Caryll Houselander*

Trying to Express Something

In the Black spiritual tradition, music is a vehicle that permits me to move from the frustration of trying to express something by inadequate means to the point where I can express something in a satisfying way, from deep down inside, comfortably and freely. Music brings me to that point. Music enables that kind of expression.

How do we know Jesus is with us? How do we know Jesus has arrived? We can feel him when he comes. And how do we get him here? By singing the words of the Lord, by praying and by putting our prayer into song, by singing and getting the spirit and beginning to feel what it is all about. And then somebody might begin to shout. People will move back and forth. They'll clap their hands. The singing will build and build and build, and people will know as surely as anyone ever could that Jesus is here.

— *Grayson Warren Brown*

We Are All Musicians

Sound and music lie at the root of our existence. There is only one story, and it is a simple one. The fundamental tone of the universe was sounded out and split itself into subtones or harmonics, until differentiation became so complex that an orchestra whose name was Babel was created. In this orchestra, the soloist, the individual player (the divine "Sol" in each of us), is required to tune himself or herself so sensitively as to be able to go back through the vibratory ramifications and to lose identity with his or her own particular and ludicrously unrelated harmonic. Further, he or she is asked to realize a dependence upon all other harmonics who, in their turn, are all related to the same One Tone. Thus, we are all musicians, whether we are bricklayers, newsvendors, scientists or poets. For the time being, whilst the music unfolds, the cosmic performance goes on. It is the musician, down here, who vicariously presents that possibility of return, and has, in the deepest sense, one of the most important roles in human life.

—*Herbert Whone*

Hallelujah!
Praise the Lord, my heart!
My whole life, give praise.
Let me sing to God
as long as I live.

—*Psalm 146:1–2*

The Cantor of the Universe

The right Hebrew word for "cantor" is *ba'al tefillah,* master of prayer. The mission of a cantor is to lead in prayer. The cantor does not stand before the Ark as an artist in isolation, trying to demonstrate skill or display vocal feats. The cantor stands before the Ark not as an individual but with a congregation.

"The heavens declare the glory of God." How do they declare it? How do they reveal it? "There is no speech, there are no words, neither is their voice heard." The heavens have no voice; the glory is inaudible. And it is the task of people to reveal what is concealed; to be the voice of the glory, to sing its silence, to utter, so to speak, what is in the heart of all things. The glory is here — invisible and silent. Man is the voice; woman is the voice; their task is to be the song. The cosmos is a congregation in need of a cantor.

Humanity is the cantor of the universe and in whose life the secret of cosmic prayer is disclosed. To sing means to sense and to affirm that the spirit is real and that its glory is present. In singing we perceive what is otherwise beyond perceiving. Song, and particularly liturgical song, is not only an act of expression but also a way of bringing down the spirit from heaven to earth.

— *Abraham Heschel*

Song and Soul

There are hardly proofs for the existence of God, but there are witnesses. Foremost among them are the Bible and music. Our liturgy is a moment in which these two witnesses come to expression. "On the evidence of two witnesses a claim is sustained." Our liturgy consists of the testimony of both music and the word. Perhaps this is the way to define *ba'al tefillah*. [The cantor] is a person in whom the two witnesses meet; a person in whom a spiritual equation takes place—the equation of song and soul, or word and mind. The self and the prayer are one.

—*Abraham Heschel*

The Most Human of Arts

Singing is the most human, most companionable of the arts. It joins us together in the whole realm of sound, forging a group identity where there were only individuals and making a communicative statement that far transcends what any one of us could do alone. It is a paradigm of union with the creator.

— *Alice Parker*

Where People Sing with Others

Singing is discovered and invented; it is born at times when there is no other possible way for people to express themselves — at the grave, for example, where four or five people with untrained, clumsy voices sing words that are greater and smaller than their faith and their experience.

A tent of meeting is a place where people sing with others. In our world there are very few other places where this happens.

— *Huub Oosterhuis*

On the Song of the Church

Why do Christians sing when they are together? The reason is, quite simply, because in singing together it is possible for them to speak and pray the same word at the same time; in other words, because here they can unite in the word.

There should be singing, not only at devotions but regular times of the day or week. The more we sing, the more joy will we derive from it, but, above all, the more devotion and discipline and joy we put into our singing, the richer will be the blessing that will come to the whole life of the fellowship from singing together.

It is the voice of the church that is heard in singing together. It is not you that sings; it is the church that is singing, and you, as a member of the church, may share in its song. Thus all singing together that is right must serve to widen our spiritual horizon, make us see our little company as a member of the great Christian Church on earth, and help us willingly and gladly to join our singing, be it feeble or good, to the song of the church.

— *Dietrich Bonhoeffer*

With Only Stubs and Knobs

June 12, 1980: The Leprosarium on Guimaras. So it was St. Alice's Day, the feast of the thirteenth-century mystic and leper. Since this feast is, appropriately enough, the patronal feast of the leprosarium, much of the day's activity in the spacious compound was being directed toward preparations for the coming feast. In one of the large barrack-wards, Sr. Marie introduced Fr. Fabian and me to some of the men who were preparing their music for the next day's celebration. There were three of them, each with his own musical instrument. The instruments themselves had been fashioned with great love, skill and ingenuity by one of the members of the trio. A musicologist would have a bit of difficulty, I admit, in classifying each of these instruments, probably settling for something generic, like "a guitar-like string instrument." But each of these musical instruments was the work of a true craftsman. What struck deepest, however, was the music itself, or rather, the musicians. I doubt that the three players had between them four whole fingers. Their hands ended mostly in knobs and stubs. What kind of music can you play with one finger, a knuckle-bone and a few stubs? Not one of the three was physically able to negotiate more than a few notes and chord-sequences. And yet, by pooling their limited resources, and by each contributing his own limited efforts, these three men were playing and singing music, *real* music, *beautiful* music. It may not have been Bach or Beethoven. But I can assure you that Bach and Beethoven would have deemed themselves privileged to join these three lepers in their music-making.

If the highly gifted (or even the moderately gifted!) individuals can exercise their gifts at liturgy for the sake of the community, splendid!

But even more important is the willingness of the rest of us, those of us with only stubs and knobs instead of fingers, to join with others like ourselves. Within such a matrix a community liturgy has every chance of flourishing.

— *Chrysogonus Waddell*

United by the Power

We are each alone. Can we all be united by the power of the song? As the first, often faint sounds come from my throat, I'm beginning to spin a web connecting me to the group, and my whole effort is to get connecting threads coming back from them. As the song builds, the thread becomes line, a rope, a cable, a bridge — and finally, there is no division. We are all one in the song.

— *Alice Parker*

Prayer of the Saints Who Make Music

We give you thanks, O God,
for all who made music before us,
playing and singing in holiness.

We thank you for Miriam, the prophet,
   who took up her tambourine
   and led Israel in song and dance
   safely on the other shore.
We thank you for David, the king,
   friend of psalm writers and singers
   whose harp soothed Saul's troubled soul.
We thank you for Deborah and for Barak,
   who sang truthfully of trials and triumphs.
With the angels who filled your Temple,
   they sing, "Holy! Holy! Holy!"

We thank you for Zechariah,
   who gave us words to sing at sunrise,
   and for Simeon,
   whose song lulls the church to sleep at night.
We thank you for Mary,
   whose Magnificat echoes through the ages

on the lips of all those
you liberate from bondage.
We thank you for the now-nameless hymnists
whose art inspired Paul to sing of Christ,
image of the invisible God
firstborn of the dead:
Jesus, the Lord!
With the angels who surprised the shepherds,
they sing "Glory! Glory! Glory!"

We thank you for Cecelia,
whose song was pure.
We thank you for Gregory
the singing bishop of Rome.
We thank you for Teresa,
dancing without shoes,
castanets in hand;
and for Rose of Lima,
whose fingers made the guitar
proclaim your praise.

We thank you for our mothers,
the first to sing to us,
for music teachers to guide us,

for organists to accompany us,
for instrumentalists to delight us,
for cantors to encourage us,
and for presiders who will chant.
May we sing together always til the
final trumpet sounds!
Then with the angels who attend your throne
with the living creatures and the elders
may we sing to you forever:
"Worthy! Worthy! Worthy!
All blessing, honor, glory and might. Amen!"

—*David Philippart*

The Song of the People

Black sacred song—old or new, folk or composed, rural or urban, traditional or contemporary—is in a very real sense, the song *of the people*.

The leader (some would say soloist) leads the community in worship. The leader revives and inspirits. The worshiping community is active, not passive. People participate—sing, pray, clap, sway, raise their hands, nod their heads. Eye contact, voiced response, the silent testimony of tears, a smile of relief or contemplation or ecstasy says, "This is my story; this is my song."

The first person pronoun, the "I" reference, is communal. The individual sings the soul of the community. In heart and voice and gesture the church, the community, responds.

— *Thea Bowman*

Lift Every Voice and Sing

Lift ev'ry voice and sing,
    till earth and heaven ring,
Ring with the harmonies of liberty;
Let our rejoicing rise high as the list'ning skies,
Let it resound as the rolling sea.
Sing a song full of the faith
that the dark past has taught us.
Sing a song full of the hope
that the present has brought us.
Facing the rising sun of our new day begun,
Let us march on till victory is won.

—*James W. Johnson*

Earth and All Stars

Earth and all stars! Loud rushing planets
Sing to the Lord a new song.
O victory! Loud shouting army
Sing to the Lord a new song!

> God has done marvelous things.
> I too, I too sing praises with a new song!

Hail, wind and rain! Loud blowing snowstorm
Sing to the Lord a new song!
Flowers and trees! Loud rustling dry leaves
Sing to the Lord a new song!

Trumpet and pipes! Loud clashing cymbals
Sing to the Lord a new song!
Harp, lute and lyre! Loud humming cellos
Sing to the Lord a new song!

Engines and steel! Loud pounding hammers
Sing to the Lord a new song!
Limestone and beams! Loud building workmen
Sing to the Lord a new song!

Classrooms and labs! Loud boiling test tubes
Sing to the Lord a new song!
Athlete and band! Loud cheering people
Sing to the Lord a new song!

Knowledge and trust! Loud sounding wisdom
Sing to the Lord a new song!
Daughter and son! Loud praying members
Sing to the Lord a new song!

— *Herbert Brokering*

With the Universe

Through singing and speaking we communicate with other humans and animals and perhaps, as in the old myths, with rocks, trees and stars. We converse with the entire universe of which we are a part. Some scientists speak of vibration as at the heart of all physical processes, so it may be literally true that "all nature sings, and round me rings, the music of the spheres" (Maltbie D. Babcock).

— *Alice Parker*

Cosmic Chorus

Once there was a time when the whole of rational creation formed a single dancing chorus looking upwards to the one leader of this dance. And the harmony of that motion which was imparted to them by reason of his law found its way into their dancing.

Our first parents still danced among the angelic powers. But the beginning of sin made an end of the sweet sounds of this chorus . . . Since then we have been deprived of this communion with the angels and, since the fall, must sweat and most arduously toil to do battle with and conquer the spirit that, thanks to sin, now weighs upon us. But the spoils of the victory will be these: that which was lost in our original defeat will once more be ours to enjoy, and once again we will take part in the dancing of the divine chorus.

—*St. Gregory of Nyssa*

The Sounding Joy

Joy to the world! The Savior reigns!
Let us our songs employ;
While fields and floods, rocks, hills and plains
Repeat the sounding joy, repeat the sounding joy
Repeat, repeat the sounding joy.

—*Isaac Watts*

When in Our Music God Is Glorified

When in our music God is glorified.
And adoration leaves no room for pride.
It is as though the whole creation cried: Alleluia!

How often, making music, we have found
A new dimension in the world of sound.
As worship moved us to a more profound
    Alleluia!

So has the church, in liturgy and song,
In faith and love, through centuries of wrong,
Borne witness to the truth in ev'ry tongue:
    Alleluia!

And did not Jesus sing a psalm that night
When utmost evil strove against the light?
Then let us sing, for whom he won the fight:
    Alleluia!

Let ev'ry instrument be tuned for praise!
Let all rejoice who have a voice to raise!
And may God give us faith to sing always:
    Alleluia!

—*Frederick Pratt Green*

Suite for Seasons

Advent

She is a reed,
Straight and simple
growing by a lake
in Nazareth.

A reed that is empty
until the breath of God
fills it with infinite music.

And the breath of the spirit of love,
utters the word of God
through an empty reed.

The word of God
is infinite music
in a little reed . . .

Mary, Mother of God,
we are the poor soil
and the dry dust,
we are hard with a cold frost . . .

Be hands that are rocking the world
to a kind rhythm of love;
that the incoherence of war
and the chaos of our unrest
be soothed to a lullaby,
And the round and sorrowful world
in your hands,
the cradle of God.

— *Caryll Houseland*

Christmas

Sing to the Lord a new song,
the Lord of wonderful deeds.
Right hand and holy arm
brought victory to God.

God made that victory known,
revealed justice to nations,

remembered a merciful love
loyal to the house of Israel.
The ends of the earth have seen
the victory of our God.

Shout to the Lord, you earth,
break into song, into praise!
Sing praise to God with a harp,
with a harp and sound of music.
With sound of trumpet and horn,
shout to the Lord, our king.

Let the sea roar with its creatures,
the world and all that live there!
Let rivers clap their hands,
the hills ring out their joy!

The Lord our God comes,
comes to rule the earth,
justly to rule the world,
to govern the peoples aright.

—*Psalm 98*

Lent

By the rivers of Babylon
we sat weeping,
remembering Zion.
There on the poplars
we hung our harps.

Our captors shouted
for happy songs,
for songs of festival.
"Sing!" they cried,
"the songs of Zion."

How could we sing
the song of the Lord
in a foreign land?

Jerusalem forgotten?
Wither my hand!
Jerusalem forgotten?
Silence my voice!
if I do not seek you
as my greatest joy.

Lord, never forget
that crime of Edom
against your city,
the day they cried,
"Strip! Smash her to the ground!"

Doomed Babylon, be cursed!
Good for those who deal you
evil for evil!
Good for those who destroy you,
who smash your children at the walls.

— *Psalm 137*

Triduum

Rejoice, heavenly powers! Sing, choirs of angels!
  Exult, all creation around God's throne!
Jesus Christ, our king, is risen!
  Sound the trumpet of salvation.

Rejoice, O earth, in shining splendor,
  radiant in the brightness of your king!
  Christ has conquered! Glory fills you!
  Darkness vanishes for ever!

Rejoice, O Mother Church! Exult in glory!
  The risen Savior shines upon you!
  Let this place resound with joy,
  echoing the mighty song of all God's people!

My dearest friends, standing with me
    in this holy light,
  join me in asking God for mercy,
  that he may give his unworthy minister
  grace to sing his Easter praises.

  — *From the* Exultet

Easter

The strains upraise of joy and praise. Alleluia!
To the glory of their king
Shall ransomed people sing, Alleluia!
And the choirs that dwell on
high shall reecho through the sky, Alleluia!
They on the fields of Paradise that roam,
The blessed ones, repeat through that bright
    home, Alleluia!
The planets glittering on their heavenly way,
The shining constellations join and say, Alleluia!
Ye clouds that onward sweep,
Ye winds on pinions light,
Ye thunders echoing loud and deep,
Ye lightnings wildly bright,—
In sweet consent unite your Alleluia!
Ye floods and ocean billows,
Ye storms and winter snow,
Ye days of cloudless beauty,
Hoar frost and summer glow,
Ye groves that wave in spring,
And glorious forest, sing Alleluia!

First let the birds with painted plumage gay
Exalt their great Creator's praise, and say Alleluia!
Then let the beasts of earth with varying strain
Join in creation's hymn and cry again, Alleluia!
Here let the mountains thunder forth sonorous,
    Alleluia!
There let the valleys sing in gentler chorus,
    Alleluia!
Thou jubilant abyss of ocean, cry Alleluia!
Ye tracts of earth and continents, reply Alleluia!
To God who all creation made,
The frequent hymn be duly paid, Alleluia!
This is the strain, the eternal strain, the Lord of
    all things loves: Alleluia!
This is the song, the heavenly song, that Christ
    himself approves: Alleluia!
Wherefore we sing, both heart and voice awaking,
    Alleluia!
And children's voices echo, answer making,
    Alleluia!
Now from all folk be outpoured
Alleluia to the Lord!
With Alleluia evermore

Suite for Seasons ▪ 39

The Son and Spirit we adore!
Praise be done to the Three in One, Alleluia!
    Alleluia!

  — *"Cantemus Cuncti Melodum," a ninth-century poem
translated by John Mason Neale*

Before a Wedding

We praise you, Lord, God of all creation,
in the festivals that gather your church
for rejoicing and prayer.
May your faithfulness strengthen the love of
 bride and groom,
your goodness and humor ready them for making
 a home.
May your promise be in the words they speak,
your joy in their gathered families,
your own song in the music we make.

May we who serve this festival with music
see the wonder of your love in every wedding
and bring from your church the song of thanks
 and blessing.
We praise you, Lord, God of all creation,
for your gift of music,
the sound of all rejoicing.

— *Gabe Huck*

When Love Is Found

When love is found and hope comes home
sing and be glad that two are one.
When love explodes, and fills the sky,
praise God and share your Maker's joy.

Praise God for love, praise God for life,
in age or youth, in husband, wife.
Lift up your hearts, let love be fed
Through death and life with broken bread.

—*Brian Wren*

Before a Funeral

Jerusalem my happy home,
    when shall I come to thee?
When shall my sorrows have an end?
    Thy joys when shall I see?

There David stands with harp in hand
    as master of the choir.
Ten thousand times we shall be blest
    that might this music hear.

Our Lady sings Magnificat
    with tune surpassing sweet;
And all the Virgins bear their parts
    sitting about her feet.

Te Deum doth Saint Ambrose sing,
    Saint Austin doth the like;
Old Simeon and Zachary
    have not their songs to seek.

There Magdalene hath left her moan
    and cheerfully doth sing
With blessed saints, whose harmony
    in ev'ry street doth ring.

—English folk ballad said to have been composed by a priest in prison in the sixteenth century

Our Rhythms Wrong

On strings untuned we pluck our own sad song
And fail to play the music you have scored.
On drums gone flat we beat our rhythms wrong;
We flail away, producing sour discord.
As our refrain we mouth the song of Cain,
The gashing, bashing, harsh and thudding sound
Of brother bringing brother death or pain,
Not displeased when another falls to ground.
But we grow tired of our discordant dirge;
We long to strike a more harmonious strain,
To orchestrate a more creative urge,
To fling, to sing the song of life again.
Spirit of love, retune our tone-deaf ears
That we may hear, and play, the music of the spheres.

—*John Combs*

Jesus said, "To what then will I compare the people of this generation, and what are they like? They are like children sitting in the marketplace and calling to one another, 'We played the flute for you, and you did not dance; we wailed, and you did not weep.'"

—*Luke 7:31–32*

Save me, Lord my God!
By day, by night, I cry out.
Let my prayer reach you;
turn, listen to me.

I am steeped in trouble,
ready for the grave.
I am like one destined for the pit,
a warrior deprived of strength,
forgotten among the dead,
buried with the slaughtered
for whom you care no more.

Lamento

You tossed me to the bottom of the pit,
into its murky darkness,
your anger pulled me down
like roaring waves.

You took my friends away,
disgraced me before them.
Trapped here with no escape,
I cannot see beyond my pain.

Lord, I cry out to you all day,
my hands keep reaching out.
Do you work marvels for the dead?
Can shadows rise and sing praise?

Is your mercy sung in the grave,
your lasting love in Sheol?
Are your wonders known in the pit,
your justice, in forgotten places?

But I cry out to you, God,
each morning I plead with you.
Why do you reject me, Lord?
Why do you hide your face?

Weak since childhood,
I am often close to death.
Your torments track me down,
your rage consumes me,
your trials destroy me.

All day, they flood around me,
pressing down, closing me in.
You took my friends from me,
darkness is all I have left.

— *Psalm 88*

Jacob's Ladder

"Through song," said the rebbe, "we climb to the highest palace. From that palace we can influence the universe and its prisons. Song is Jacob's ladder forgotten on earth by the angels. Sing and you shall defeat death; sing and you shall disarm the foe."

— *Elie Weisel*

When From Death I'm Free

And when from death I'm free, I'll sing on,
    I'll sing on.
And when from death I'm free, I'll sing on.
And when from death I'm free, I'll sing and
    joyful be,
And through eternity, I'll sing on, I'll sing on
And through eternity, I'll sing on.

   — *Alexander Means*

Blessing of Musicians

God of glory,
your beloved Son has shown us
that true worship comes from humble
    and contrite hearts.

Bless our brothers and sisters,
who have responded to the needs of our parish
and wish to commit themselves to your service
as musicians.

Grant that their ministry may be fruitful
and our worship pleasing in your sight.
We ask this through Christ our Lord.

—*Book of Blessings*

Blessing of the Church Bell

Lord, bless this bell
that has been made to call the children
    of the church.
May the ringing of this bell scatter the forces of
    treachery, the shadow of shadows, the ruin
    of storms.
May the bell's sound be our call to prayer.
Held here in the arms of our mother, our church,
we shall sing to you a new song:
in the blast of the trumpet,
the gentle rhythms of the dulcimer,
the harmony of the organ,
the beat of the drum,
the joy of the cymbal.
So shall our song summon to this place
    of your glory
a multitude of angels.

—*Adapted from the old Roman Pontifical*

Blessing of an Organ

With hands outstretched the celebrant says the prayer of blessing:

Lord God, your beauty is ancient yet ever new,
your wisdom guides the world in right order,
and your goodness gives the world
    its variety and splendor.
The choirs of angels join together
to offer their praise by obeying your commands.
The galaxies sing your praises
by the patterns of their movement
that follow your law.
The voices of the redeemed join
    in a chorus of praise
to your holiness as they sing to you
    in mind and heart.
We your people, joyously gathered in this church,
wish to join our voices
    to the universal hymn of praise.
So that our song may rise more worthily
    to your majesty,
we present this organ for your blessing:

grant that its music may lead us
to express our prayer and praise
in melodies that are pleasing to you.
We ask this through Christ our Lord. Amen.

Then the celebrant places incense in the censer and incenses the organ, as the organ is played for the first time.

— Book of Blessings

Music Is Ministry

Among the many signs and symbols used by the church to celebrate its faith, music is of preeminent importance. As sacred song united to the words, it forms an integral part of solemn liturgy. Yet the function of music is ministerial; it must serve and never dominate. Music should assist the assembled believers to express and share the gift of faith that is within them and to nourish and strengthen their interior commitment of faith. It should heighten the texts so that they speak more fully and more effectively. The quality of joy and enthusiasm which music adds to community worship cannot be gained in any other way. It imparts a sense of unity to the congregation and sets the appropriate tone for a particular celebration.

Music, in addition to expressing texts, can also unveil a dimension of meaning and feeling, a communication of ideas and intuitions which words alone cannot yield.

—*Bishops' Committee on the Liturgy*

After the Liturgy

"Sing to the Lord a new song. Sing praise in the assembly of the saints."

My dear children, fruit of the true faith and holy seed of heaven, all you who have been born again in Christ and whose life is from above, listen to me. Or rather, listen to the Holy Spirit saying through me: "Sing to the Lord a new song." Look, you tell me, I am singing. Yes, you are singing, you are singing clearly. I can hear you. Make sure that your life does not contradict your song. Sing with your voices, your hearts, your lips and your lives. Sing to the Lord a new song.

You wish to know what praises to sing? The answer is: "God's praise is in the assembly of the saints." It is in the singers themselves! If you desire to praise God, then live what you express. Live good lives and you yourselves will be his praise.

—*Saint Augustine*

Are There Still Lullabies?

Are there still lullabies that parents sing to their children? Are there catchy nursery rhymes and things like the alphabet song and "eency weency spider"? (If you think repetition isn't powerful, stop right here and sing that spider song—with the gestures!) Are there school songs? Parodies of school songs? Jump rope songs? Camp songs? Are there work songs? Prison songs? Are there Christmas carols that get sung in homes? Are there protest songs sung by the people who protest?

It is not only this one ritual of ours—Sunday eucharist—that has its music, that must be sung. All sorts of regular moments, recurring moments, have had their tunes, their sounds. Do they still? Do they have these not as nostalgia and not as entertainment but as their own, as the very way we rock a baby, walk a picket line, begin a morning, end a year, keep a festival? Are we losing the habit of song in a world crammed full of music?

—*Gabe Huck*

Praise! Praise God in the temple,
in the highest heavens!
Praise! Praise God's mighty deeds
and noble majesty.

Praise! Praise God with trumpet blasts,
with lute and harp.
Praise! Praise God with timbrel and dance,
with strings and pipes.

Praise! Praise God with crashing cymbals,
with ringing cymbals.
All that is alive, praise. Praise the Lord.
Hallelujah!

—*Psalm 150*